Eva Hoffman

For You, Dear Teacher

Illustrations by Justina Langley

Learn to Learn

To my father, Jan Hoffman, whose life-long passion
for learning and teaching, boundless positive energy
and enthusiasm for life have always inspired me
and greatly influenced all my endeavours.

To Peter Wingard, my wonderful friend and mentor,
a truly exceptional human being.
Peter's wisdom, modesty, genuine respect for people,
his never-ending desire to learn, and share his
knowledge with others, and his ability to enjoy life have
added so much light and joy to mine.

Published by LEARN TO LEARN

PO Box 29
Middlewich
CW10 9FN - UK
Tel +44 (0)1606 832 895
Fax +44 (0)1606 837 645
learntolearn@connectfree.co.uk
www.learntolearn.org.uk

Printed in England

My thanks go to

all the teachers who have generously shared their

experience with me, attended my workshops, and through

discussions contributed greatly to the content of this book;

to my wonderful friends - Susan Norman, Richard Kirby

and Fay Wertheimer, for reading the manuscript

and making valuable comments and corrections.

If you are thinking a year ahead,
    sow a seed.

If you are thinking ten years ahead,
    plant a tree.

If you are thinking a hundred years ahead,
    teach children.

(Chinese anon. 500 BC)

For You,
Dear Teacher

from

Eva Hoffman
words

Justina Langley
pictures

invite change into your life

live your life to the full

for You dear Teacher

5

6

1 From my ♡ to yours

4 when life gets tough

3

2 cherish who you are

protect your integrity

Contents

FROM MY HEART TO YOURS

Dear Teacher,

Have you ever had days when
   walking into a classroom requires an act of will,
   you can hardly remember why you became a teacher in the first place,
   all your enthusiasm for teaching seems to have vanished,
   on Monday morning you are already longing for Friday afternoon?
I certainly have, and so has every teacher I have ever met.

No matter how much we love our work and how much we care about children, many of us go through spells of feeling helpless, inadequate, and disillusioned… However, having been brought up in a culture which believes in gritting our teeth and getting on with it, we hate admitting we need help, support, understanding and appreciation.

You may choose to do nothing and wait until it is time to retire and risk feeling more and more bitter and disillusioned. You may decide the time has come to leave the profession and make a new start elsewhere. Alternatively, you may embark on a journey which will remind you that there is MUCH more to teaching than just enduring it, a journey that may rekindle your joy and your enthusiasm.

There is always a choice.
Having been a teacher for a very long time, I have had many ups and many downs. I have experienced both enthusiasm and excitement, as well as feelings of inadequacy and frustration. Still, I would never want to have done anything else with my life. I hope you will find in this book a large dose of genuine understanding and a great deal of sympathy and empathy.
However you feel at the moment, I would like to invite you to take a closer look at your options. Give yourself permission to spend some time with this important person in your life, YOU.
You owe it to yourself !

I have written this book

to guide you towards appreciating and being proud of
who you are and of what you do,

to help you validate your thoughts and your feelings,
and to reassure you that you are not alone,

to bring to your awareness the importance of your well-being
and point out ways in which you can help yourself,

to help you find your way of functioning in the world of targets,
measurements and other external pressures,

to uplift you, motivate you, and to encourage you
to live your life to the full.

Teaching is sacred

As teachers we are significant people in our pupils' lives. This gives us great power as well as enormous responsibility. We have the power to change people's lives and the responsibility to guide their minds and hearts, helping them towards becoming the best they are capable of becoming.

We have no way of knowing how far the influence of what we do will go or how many generations it will affect.

Teaching is unique

Whatever we teach filters through our whole being: our soul, our heart, our mind and our body.

Teaching involves all parts of the unique instrument - You. The quality of the instrument, the material of which it is made, its shape and balance, the fine-tuning and its soul, all determine the quality of the sound it makes. That is why taking good care of the instrument is so crucial.

Teaching makes us vulnerable

Teaching is giving - from the mind, from the heart, from our essence, and through our bodies. Giving of our whole selves by exposing who we are makes us an easy target for hurt and disappointment.

The expectations of our profession are enormous and keep increasing while the support we receive does not. Teacher bashing has become a favourite pastime of the media, some government officials and sections of the general public. It is not surprising we frequently feel terribly isolated, undervalued, unappreciated and disillusioned.

Teaching can be enormously frustrating

The complexity of the children with whom we work, their in many cases difficult circumstances combined with the pressure to achieve, measure up, and reach targets, could drive anybody insane. However, the greatest frustration comes from our inner struggle to remain true to ourselves, to preserve our integrity. This task is made more difficult whenever we are expected to do things we consider wrong and even harmful to the children. As if that weren't enough, we find every Tom, Dick, and Harry relishing any opportunity to tell us where we go wrong and what we ought to do.

Isn't it just maddening?!

You may sometimes feel uncomfortably 'pushed' when reading this book and doing the exercises. Don't let it discourage you from looking carefully and deeply into the important person, You.

Everything you find on the pages of this book comes from my heart with the intention of reaching yours.

CHERISH WHO YOU ARE

Who you are makes a difference

A Rabbi was once asked what he thought the kingdom of God would be like.

I don't know - he replied. *But one thing I do know. When I get there I am not going to be asked, 'Why weren't you Moses?' I am going to be asked, 'Were you fully You?'*

I would like to invite you to spend some time exploring the person at the centre of your private universe, namely You. Allow yourself to stop and take time to think so that you can become more aware of your roles, your dreams, needs, values and beliefs and how they affect your life.

Our extremely busy lives make it only too easy for us to lose sight of ourselves. We are a giving, caring and nurturing profession but in nurturing others' hearts, minds, souls and bodies we forget that we ourselves are people in our own right. We forget that the quality of our selfhood forms the way in which we relate not only to ourselves but also to others.

Knowing others is intelligence,
Knowing yourself is wisdom.

(anon)

My true self, the essence of me
is my uniqueness
and the ultimate gift I can offer
to people with whom I come into contact.

I am prepared to take the risk
and tell people who I really am.

Everything I teach is linked to,
reflects and depends on who I am.

WHAT MAKES YOU WHO YOU ARE ?

Jot down your thoughts in the cloud...

In answering the question you may have included
some of the following:

    your appearance
    the sound of your voice
            your likes and dislikes
            your personality traits
    your strengths and weaknesses
    the roles you play in life
            your needs
            your dreams
    values you hold
    your genetic make-up
            the people who raised you
            the culture in which you were raised
    the important people who influenced you
    your life experiences - loves, pains, passions, responsibilities, events
            the lessons you have learned from your experiences
            the good and ill your have done to yourself and others

In this book we will focus only on a few aspects of your identity.

However, use the next page to create a full picture of who you are.

MY IDENTITY - ALL ABOUT ME

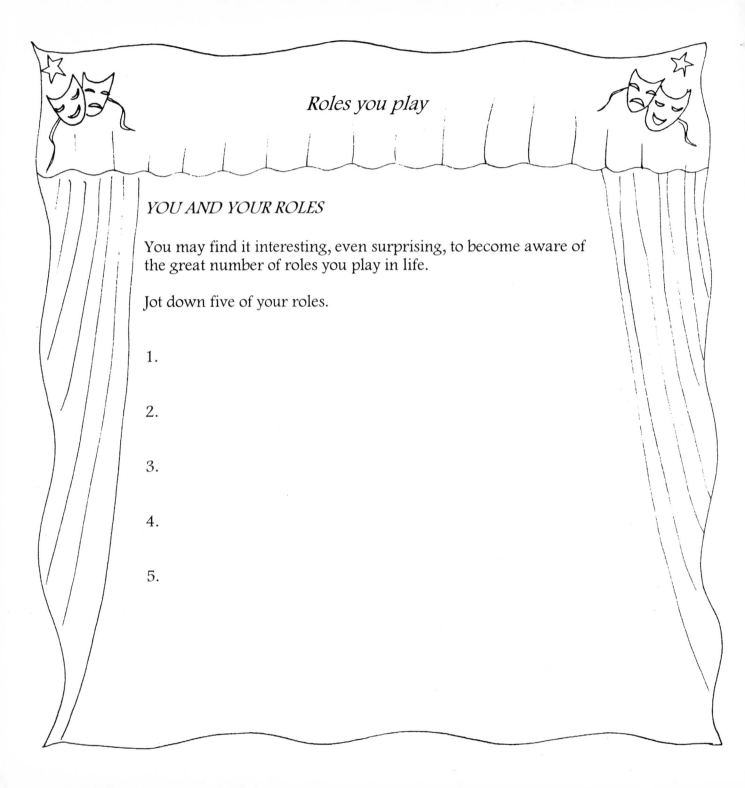

Roles you play

YOU AND YOUR ROLES

You may find it interesting, even surprising, to become aware of the great number of roles you play in life.

Jot down five of your roles.

1.

2.

3.

4.

5.

and now five more

6.

7.

8.

9.

10.

and another five

11.

12.

13.

14.

15.

any more?

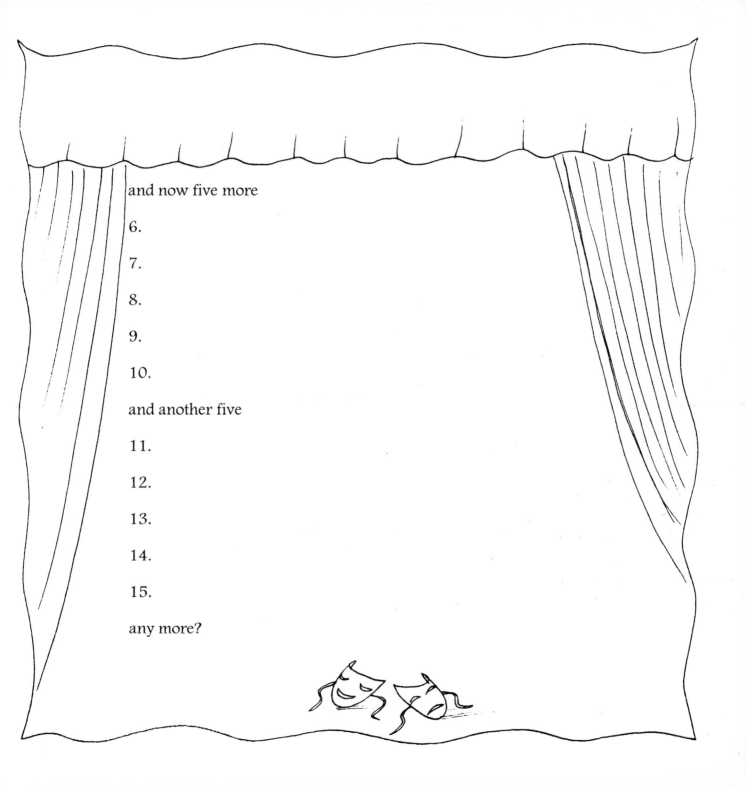

Being a teacher is only one of many roles in your life.

1. Do you see yourself acting a role, i.e. pretending you are somebody you are not, wearing a mask, acting as if you were somebody else?

2. Do you see yourself interacting with others in a way appropriate to the people and the situations, from that 'authentic' part of yourself?

How are the two ways of understanding roles different?

What difference, if any, does it make to those with whom you interact?

The roles we play require different skills, emotional engagement, actions and attitudes.

Go back to the previous page and mark which of your roles require the following:

1. caring / nurturing / loving
2. full attention / thinking / solving problems
3. knowledge / skills / learning
4. flexibility / understanding
5. patience / acceptance / tolerance
6. great amount of energy

Look again at your list and think:

Which are the most important roles you play?

Which are the most demanding?

Most enjoyable?

Most rewarding?

You can now see with clarity how incredibly demanding many of your roles are.
No matter how important, rewarding or enjoyable your role as a teacher may be and how much you identify with it, it is obvious there is more to you than being a teacher.

Look in the mirror and say to yourself:

Being a teacher is ONE of my roles!

Avoid over-identifying with your roles - it can be risky, sometimes even dangerous.

You are not your roles! At any moment in life you may choose to shed or add a role to your repertoire, e.g. become a parent or a writer.

How much of the real you do you present to your pupils, and how much of your role as a teacher is a pure show?

Discussing it with a friend may clarify your thoughts on the subject.

You and your dreams

you've got to have a dream…
…to make it come true…

When did you last talk to somebody about your dreams?

When we are young we imagine the world we want to live in, things we
want to have, things we want to achieve and places we want to see.
Many people never stop dreaming about these things.
Some of us may, however, feel hurt or disappointed by the way life has
turned out and give up dreaming. We may give up wanting things to
happen, believing this will protect us from more disappointment and hurt.
We close our hearts, freeze our souls and await retirement. How very sad.
Life hardly ever turns out the way we plan it but this is not a reason to give
up dreaming.

Revive your dreams! They will probably be different from the ones you had
a few years ago but as you re-discover the power of dreams, you may well
get a new lease of life.

Do you remember what you used to dream about when you were a child?

And ten years later?

Rekindle your dreams

What are your dreams now? If you haven't got many at the moment, invent them. It may sound outrageous but it is a good start!

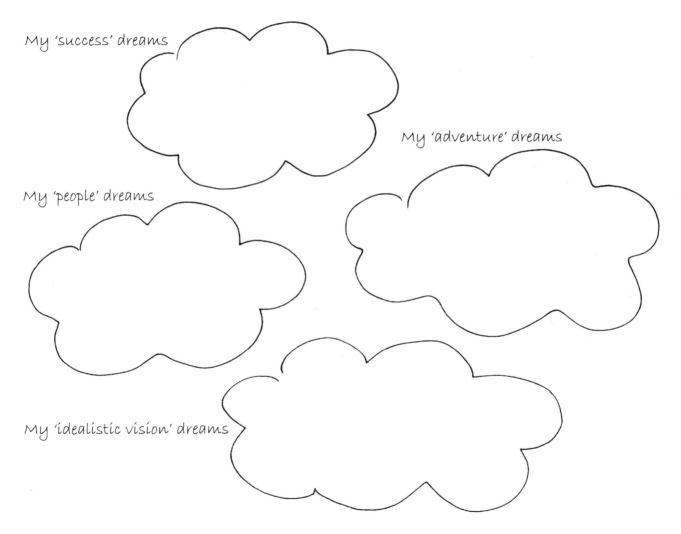

My 'success' dreams

My 'adventure' dreams

My 'people' dreams

My 'idealistic vision' dreams

Do you have a dream regarding your work ?

You and your needs

We spend our lives attending to the needs of others: our young children, our older children, (always children!) our husbands, wives or partners, our parents, our relatives, our friends, neighbours, colleagues and most importantly OUR PUPILS. We spend a great deal of time either teaching or thinking about teaching, deliberating how to satisfy the diverse needs of the youngsters in our care.

When was the last time somebody asked you about your needs?

When was the last time you stopped and asked yourself what your needs are?

Put the book down, look at yourself in the mirror and ask yourself NOW -
WHAT ARE MY NEEDS?

Write your needs on the bare branches in the picture.

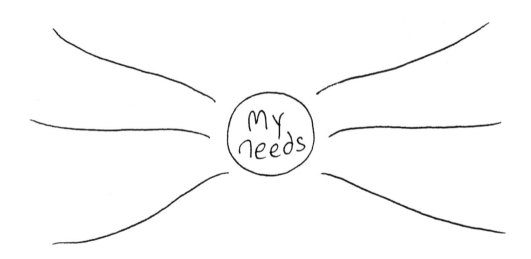

MORE ABOUT YOUR NEEDS

We are supposed to send our students on an enjoyable journey of discovery and learning. Is the joy of discovery and learning a part of Your life?

What do You need to make the joy of learning a part of Your life?

We want children to develop a feeling of self-worth. Yet, how good do You feel about Yourself?

What do You need to feel better about Yourself?

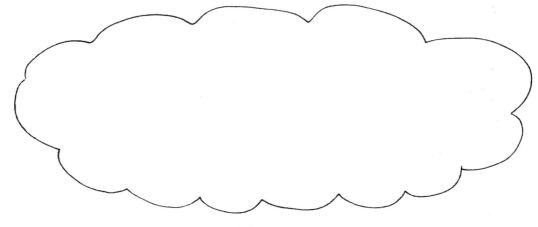

We want children to become confident life-long learners. Can you call yourself a confident life-long learner?

What do you need to be more confident about your learning?

As teachers, we try to relate to the whole student - mind, body, emotions and spirit.

Do you treat yourself as a whole person? Do you respect, care about and give enough consideration to all parts of you?

What do you need to relate better to yourself?

How does thinking about YOUR needs make you feel?

Many teachers with whom I work talk about feeling extreme discomfort. Some express feelings of sadness, anger, guilt and frustration. Many are tearful, saying it is the first time they have ever been asked to think about their needs. A few people didn't even want to think about their needs. *If I think about it, I'll never stop crying*, is what I hear teachers say over and over again. Life without having one's needs met is often reduced to mere survival.

Whatever your needs are, they are valid and important.

You may need freedom to express your views and to do what you profoundly believe is right. You may need time alone, just time to be. You may need respect from those around you, appreciation, love and caring. You may need to be listened to, to laugh and have fun.

Jack Canfield* suggests you learn the following sentences by heart and say them to your reflection in the mirror:

My needs are as important as my children's needs.

My needs are as important as my husband's/wife's needs.

My needs are as important as my parents' needs.

My needs are as important as my pupils' needs.

My needs are as important as my friends' needs.

When you do it for the first time it may feel awkward, extremely uncomfortable, even scary. You may feel guilty that you are becoming egotistical or self-centred. If this is the case, just remember you are not claiming that your needs are more important than anybody else's. All you are saying that they are NOT LESS IMPORTANT. What can be wrong with that?

Would you tell your child or your close friend she should forget about herself, neglect her own mind, body and soul, ignore her needs and lose herself in the service of others?

Be your own good friend and treat yourself as you treat your friends.

As Jack Canfield* says: *If you treated your friends the way you treat yourself, would you have any?* For many of us the answer is: *probably not...*

Are you taking care of
yourself?

If not, why not?

You can't pour water out of an empty vessel, goes an old saying. When our reserves are low and we stubbornly continue to give, we put ourselves under tremendous stress. Constant stress depletes our energy resources and blocks the energy flow. When we don't stop to clear the energy pathways, we are in danger of 'overheating the engine'. It's like driving a car at full speed with the handbrake on. If we ignore the frantically flashing red lights and press on - we break down.

And then we feel taken for granted, angry and resentful. We have been doing so much and nobody seems to appreciate it.

It makes sense to remember that everybody, our children, our students, our partners, friends and colleagues easily get used to taking as much from us as they can. That is human nature and you will be wise to accept this fact. Probably nobody will notice you are running out of steam so don't expect it and don't count on it.

It is up to YOU to stop the downward spiral of self-destruction and start taking care of yourself. It is up to you to let people know the time has come for you to take care of YOUR needs and re-charge YOUR batteries. It is up to you to ask for help and ask others to meet your needs.

BALANCING YOUR LIFE

Here is a little exercise - an adaptation of Jack Black's 'Wheel of Life' I found many years ago in his book, 'Mind Store'. I have since used it many times myself and encouraged many generations of students and teachers to do so.

My Wheel of Life

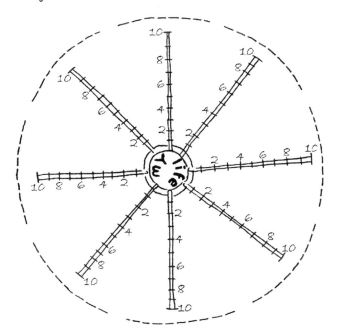

The wheel has eight spokes. Select eight important aspects of your life and write them on the lines outside the wheel. Using the scale marks, give yourself a grade showing how well you thing you are doing in this area. Join your numbers together to see how your circle of life is turning round.

Here are a few examples of some 'important aspects' of people's lives: health, family, spirituality, self-development, community work, finances, relationship, friendships, career, social life.

How much of a circle is your wheel?

What thoughts and feeling has this exercise evoked in you?
I find this to be a powerful way of revealing to me the truth about the way I live.
It gives me a clearer picture of what is going well and what areas need attention.

You and your values

Many years ago professor of philosophy Anwar Dil was a visiting lecturer at the university where I was teaching. To give his students an insight into the importance of values, professor Dil organised a panel debate: 'My Value System and How It Affects My Life'. He invited a number of lecturers and administrators to participate in the debate. I happened to be one of them. The audience was to be made up of our students, people who knew us well - no chance to bluff, even if any of us were tempted to!
The prospect made me so anxious I found some feeble excuse not to attend.

But the following summer professor Dil was back, and this time nothing could save me from taking part in the panel discussion...
I was already a seasoned teacher at the time but believe me, the debate was the most challenging presentation I have ever done in my entire life. Preparing my presentation taught me a lot about myself and was a truly unforgettable experience at the same time.

Ever since that memorable summer I have been inviting my students and colleagues to bring their value system into their awareness. While they work on theirs, I go through the process myself, observing with great interest how my priorities change and how certain values never lose their unquestionable importance.

Our values are of great importance because from them springs our belief system which is responsible for the way we act in life. It is the quality of our thinking that determines how constructive, informed and wise our beliefs will be. While our values may remain unchanged, our beliefs will reflect our growth, maturity and evolving wisdom.

Here is an example of a value and possible resulting beliefs:

Tolerating differences in thinking and opinions is the key to successful relationships

Tolerance is the absolute prerequisite of peace

Embracing diversity is the main purpose of education

Tolerance

We need to understand people's motives

We need to accept people's behaviour

We should do away with punishing offenders

We need to allow children to freely express their feelings

Let me give you another example:
If one of your values is having money, you probably believe that *in order to be happy and consider yourself successful you need to have plenty of money* . This belief may lead you towards getting good qualifications, choosing a lucrative profession, looking for connections in the rich circles, conforming to your parents' wishes to avoid being disinherited, or working extremely hard to make the desired pots of gold. Nothing really dreadful - so far.

However, if your belief were: *in order to be happy and feel successful I need to have plenty of money, whatever it takes -* you are on a dangerous path to opportunism and corruption.

Since your behaviours stem from your beliefs, in order to change your behaviour you would need to change your beliefs. Not necessarily your values!
Lets go back to the 'money' value. If the belief stemming from it is:
In order to be happy I need to have enough money (rather than 'plenty of money') - you might not need to conform to your parents' wishes and do something you hate doing. Should your parents refuse to give you money, you will make it some other way. The difference between 'plenty' and 'enough' is very significant.

Have you ever given yourself a chance to seriously think about your value system and to create a comprehensive picture of it?

Let me invite you to go through this fascinating process of self-discovery. It would be useful if you included some values connected with your professional life.

Below is a skeleton mind map: on the thick branches write your values and on the thinner ones write some of your beliefs resulting from them.

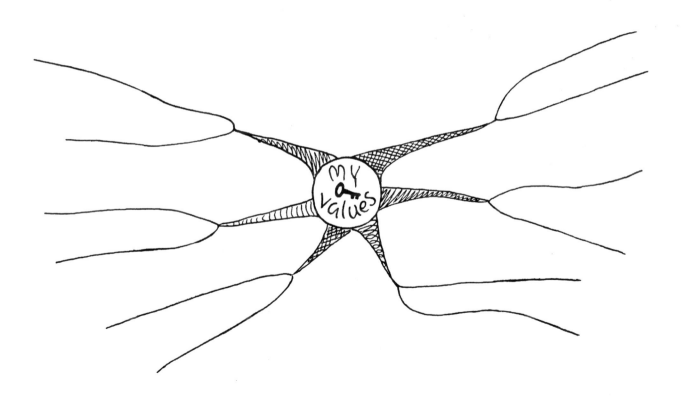

You and your roots

Your roots have played an important part in shaping your identity. Some of us dislike our roots, feel ashamed of them and consequently try to forget about them, flatly refusing to give them serious consideration.

Your values may be identical, similar or completely different from those with which you grew up. Whichever is true for you, it is still good to remember that nothing can diminish the important role your roots played in your personal growth.

Disowning your roots, running away from them or denying their existence will work against you and you may well find yourself lost, feeling shaky and uncertain who you really are.

Be grateful to your roots for feeding you and allowing you to grow, even if they didn't seem helpful at the time. It may be necessary to forgive people from your past so that you can move on.
One way or another, your roots deserve your acknowledgement.

How do you feel about your roots?

You and your vital life experiences

Every experience shapes us in some way but some of the most important experiences have a dramatic impact on our identity.
To bring your important experiences to your awareness, list them under the following headings:

significant events

opportunities

your work

changes

music

crises

jobs

art

films

books

career

education

challenges

important people

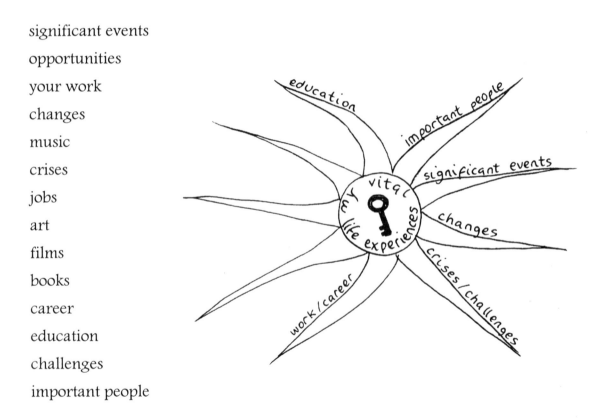

Consider how these experiences have formed the person you are today.
What have you learned from them?

WRITE ABOUT ONE OF THE KEY LIFE EXPERIENCES THAT HAS CHANGED YOUR LIFE

If appropriate, take this opportunity to thank people who played an important role in this vital life lesson.

APPRECIATION

Have you ever met someone who appreciates her uniqueness, appreciates who she is and yet is miserable, permanently angry or unhappy?

Have you met a person who would be truly appreciative of what he has and who he is and yet be unhappy, permanently angry and miserable?

Would you like to become more appreciative? You could start today by making a list of things for which you are grateful in your life.

what I appreciate...

...about my work

...about my family

...about being alive

...about my personality

...about my friends

Many of us have difficulties with giving appreciation to ourselves.

Take a couple of deep breaths and answer the two questions:

1. What have I recently done that I can be proud of?

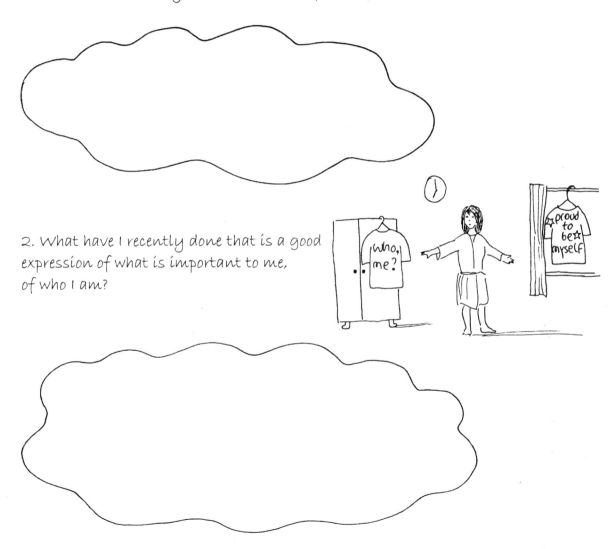

2. What have I recently done that is a good expression of what is important to me, of who I am?

When you appreciate what you have
and focus on abundance,
your life feels abundant.

When you focus on lack,
your life will feel lacking.

It is your decision, your choice.

Write about a classroom success
you are pleased with and proud of.

And another one:

And one more:

my truth and I

PROTECT YOUR INTEGRITY

How we feel about ourselves depends, among other things, on whether or not we act in agreement with our values.

You spend a vast amount of your time teaching, talking about teaching or learning, learning about teaching or learning, preparing your lessons, classes, lectures or presentations. Your life revolves around teaching, hence your way of looking at and understanding learning and teaching are an intrinsic part of who you are.

YOU AND YOUR VERY OWN PHILOSOPHY OF EDUCATION

Forget every definition you've ever heard and jot down your own thoughts about the purpose and meaning of education.
Put your ideas in the 'clouds'.

For me, education is about...

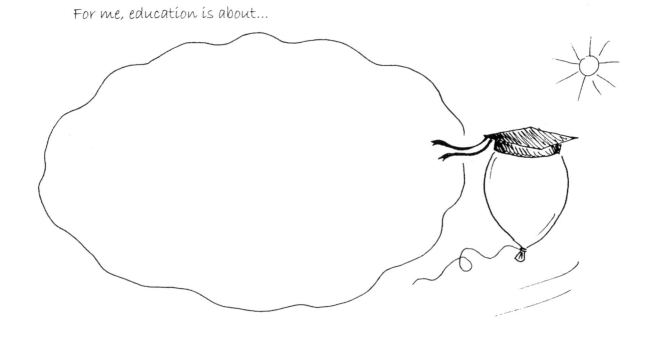

PRACTISING WHAT WE PREACH

Now take a look at your notes, think for a moment, and ask yourself a few questions:

What have I recently done that expresses what is truly important to me?

What have I recently been doing that does not reflect my values and beliefs?

What are the educational values truly close to my heart that I cannot and will not compromise?

Compromising seems to be the key to a relatively peaceful life. We make compromises every day in every aspect of our daily existence. Can you imagine life without compromises? Sounds like the most nightmarish horror story! And yet, how often do we suddenly realise that we have gone too far, that we have compromised too much, that we are beginning to lose sight of what we really are about? Whether you have experienced it or not, imagine the feelings that accompany this kind of realisation.

When asked about their feelings arising from lack of harmony between what is imposed on them and what they believe in, many teachers express sadness, frustration, resentment, bitterness, and anger.

It is natural to protect and defend one's ego. Many of us, in order to avoid feeling the pain of disappointment with ourselves, modify our beliefs or quieten the inner voice. In an attempt to convince ourselves and the world that everything is well and under control, we become alienated, distant, seemingly indifferent, or hardened and pompous.

Have you ever heard yourself sound pompous, distant, irritable or hostile when talking to your students, your pupils, their parents or your colleagues? Have you walked past them with an air of superiority or an expression:
I am too busy to notice you?
If so, what do you think brought this about?
Was that an act of defence?
Against what?

Compromising one's integrity doesn't always happen overnight. It often creeps in slowly, gradually changing our way of thinking, sometimes with devastating effects.

The well known 'frog story' illustrates the point. Throw a frog into very hot water and no doubt it will sense the danger and immediately try to jump out. Put the same frog into cold water and then slowly, very slowly, keep heating the water up, the frog will gradually get used to higher temperature. It may not notice the moment when the water becomes just that much too hot...!

The same happens to us. We come fresh to the teaching profession. We come full of enthusiasm, sensitive to what really counts and what we expect we will achieve. If the environment we encounter is not what we expected, we want to get out of it - and some of us do. Most schools, however, have something that attracts us: a kind head, pleasant colleagues, convenient location... so we stay. As time goes by, we get used to the imposed way of thinking, to the educational bureaucrats' 'speak', to measuring the immeasurable and satisfying the requirements of those in authority, no matter how outrageous they may appear to us. After all, we need our jobs, we need to earn a living and most of us love teaching and love our students.

Being a part of a system may sometimes require bending your values. You may be tempted to ignore your inner voice signalling that your compromising has gone too far.

It doesn't feel comfortable to be constantly reminded about what we really believe in but our inner voice does everything it can to make itself heard. The incongruence between what you believe in and what you practise violates your soul.

How would you recognise symptoms of integrity under threat? Jot down any ideas you may have.

Your integrity is certainly under threat when you notice that more and more frequently you give up on your students, on your superiors, on the system; when you feel resigned, powerless, and distant; when you just put on a show (the best you can under the circumstances) and can't wait for Friday.

Lack of integrity destroys our self-image, results in negativity, complaining, cynicism, constant criticism of just about everything. It brings stress, which may cause burnout, depression and any kind of physical illness. It makes you suppress your real Self and go into 'survival mode'. You lose your spark, your joy and enthusiasm. You settle for: *Nothing I do will make a difference anyway, I just have to plod along.*

Have you been there? I have, and I know how profoundly destructive the survival mode is. It takes all your energy away, and slowly but surely eats you up.

Your experience of 'survival mode'
(jot down your thoughts)

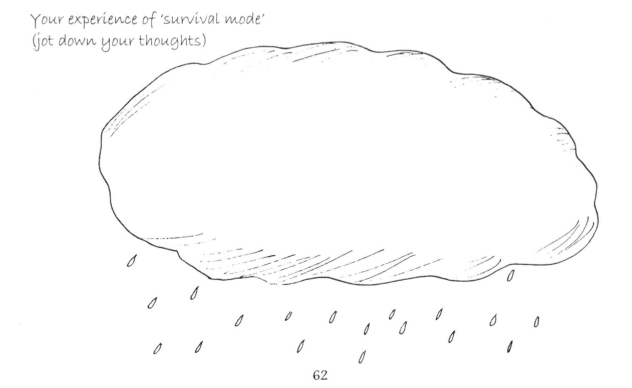

62

The realisation of what is happening to us comes in different ways. For some of us it may be a slowly growing awareness. Others wake up one morning startled by the realisation of what is going on in their lives. When that moment comes and the gap between their values and their actions becomes intolerable, their life reaches a crossroads.

The choice is obvious but far from simple: we may decide to leave school and look for another way of earning a living, or we may decide to *bring our actions into harmony with our inner life* (P. J. Palmer*). Palmer describes the process as finding a new centre for our life, a centre that is not linked with the school, with the educational system and its demands.

Whatever decision you make, whether you opt in or out of the system, do remember that your value as a person remains untouched. Just bearing in mind that you have a choice may be truly liberating in your present situation.

OVERHEATED FROGS
SURVIVAL HELPLINE

You – a private person, You – a professional:

two separate identities or '2 in 1'?

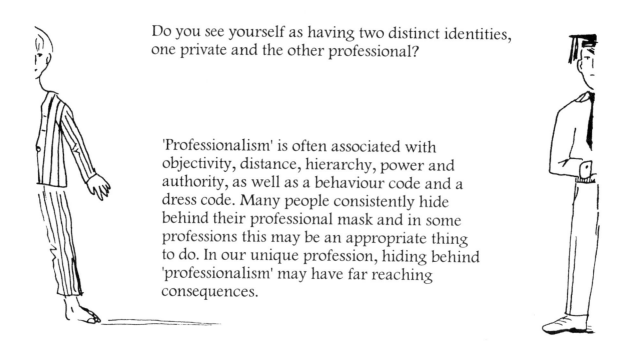

Do you see yourself as having two distinct identities, one private and the other professional?

'Professionalism' is often associated with objectivity, distance, hierarchy, power and authority, as well as a behaviour code and a dress code. Many people consistently hide behind their professional mask and in some professions this may be an appropriate thing to do. In our unique profession, hiding behind 'professionalism' may have far reaching consequences.

We may choose to hide our true selves because of all kinds of insecurities (I will lose my authority and power if I show who I am), fears (nobody must know that I make mistakes or that I don't know all the answers), or shame (I didn't do well at school, or don't want people to know my family background). Acting on insecurities, fears, shame, combined with poor self-esteem, leads to the need to pretend all the time and in all situations. Not a good place to be and, in spite of the safety motives, not a safe one either.

Pretence is a potential troublemaker because while it may fool some adults, it will never fool children. Your students can see through you from the moment you walk into the room. Despite their youth and lack of experience, they are careful observers and a sensitive audience.

For us who teach, who give our minds, hearts, and souls to our students, the division into a professional and a private person is not desirable, probably not possible. If it is true that we teach who we are, which of me is the one I teach to the children?
In the common concept of 'Professional Me' there is my mind, my sense of responsibility, my knowledge and skills, the codes, my power and authority. However, there is hardly any place for any heart-felt caring, genuine empathy, love, the 'Real Me' with my values and attitudes, my strengths and my weaknesses.

Authenticity is a great asset in relating to people, particularly the young people we teach. Again, if it is true that we teach who we are, and I truly believe we do, isn't it educationally sound for the 'I' who comes in contact with the students to be the 'authentic I', who admits to making mistakes, who doesn't seek power over others, who can accept myself for who I am? Or is it the 'I' who builds a protective layer of defences, hiding my insecurities behind a mask of power, the system, or so called 'professionalism'?

We can work on our insecurities, work towards raising our self esteem, towards feeling comfortable with who we are, work on our tolerance and accept that mistakes are an indispensable part of learning. Alternatively, we can perpetuate the pretence game, be hard on the outside but insecure, vulnerable, and quite often miserable on the inside; or even worse, we can reach the stage where we are no longer sure who we really are.

When we develop as teachers,
our horizons expand:
with everything we learn, we change
and ultimately grow as people.

When we grow as people,
our acceptance and understanding
of ourselves and others deepen:
with everything we learn, we change
and ultimately become better teachers.

In our profession one can hardly happen
without the other and the dividing line
between a private person and a
professional is barely visible.

Re-connecting with your Self

Being honest

Having been raised in a culture where independence, being strong and able to cope 'no matter what' are held in high esteem, many of us have a serious difficulty admitting we have a problem.
Why? There is hardly anything we fear more than being accused of incompetence.

Many of us tell children it's OK to make mistakes as long as they learn from them; we tell our pupils that nobody is perfect and that they just need to do their best and make progress. And yet we feel that in our jobs there is no place for mistakes and that, if we are not perfect, we are failing. This is a sure recipe for a miserable life.

Definitely a mistake!

The need to be perfect can make your life hell.
How about settling for always doing your best
and working on getting better?

Do you know anybody who doesn't make mistakes?

How do you treat the mistakes of others?

Do you make it clear to the children that it is OK to make
mistakes as long as they learn from them?

Do you tell colleagues that mistakes happen to us all and that
there is no need to worry?

What do you tell yourself when you have made a mistake?
Are you kind and understanding or critical and judgmental?

Admitting that you are not perfect, that you have made a mistake,
that you don't know all the answers, that you yourself are doing
your best to learn, is the most profoundly liberating experience.
I have discovered it for myself and have met many people in our
profession who have chosen the path of honest authenticity.

Some great teachers I have met have shown the courage to share their feelings and fears openly with their pupils, with their pupils' parents and with their colleagues.

I was once wholeheartedly congratulating a teacher on the wonderful job I believed she was doing. *Thank you*, she said, *it's good to be appreciated. But believe me, there are times when I feel totally inadequate!*
I also remember a day when I overheard a teacher saying to her class: *I am extremely angry and very upset but it has nothing to do with you. Please bear with me and it will soon pass.*

When you have a bad day you can try telling your students about it. Children, young and older, will understand. They may even help you get through the day and they will get an important message that it's fine to let others know how they feel.

For many of us sharing our feelings works really well. It means allowing your students to see and accept the real you.

Being authentic may not always bring the expected positive result but for many of us it can be a wonderfully liberating experience, one which has the potential of helping us feel connected to our pupils. And what a wonderful feeling that is!

If you haven't done it yet, take a risk: choose the right moment and try it. If you have, describe your experience on the next page.

My experience of sharing my feelings with my students

Asking for help when you need it

Bill Rogers* believes *too often teachers do not seek help because it feels like an admission of incompetence; and they do not offer it because it feels like accusing a colleague of incompetence.* Does that ring true?

For many task-oriented, ambitious teachers, coping and being strong is a matter of pride; they need to prove to the world, as well as to themselves, that one way or another they can manage in any circumstances.

There are schools where teachers feel safe to admit they need help. There are others, however, where admitting one is not coping and asking for support is a serious risk.

To which group does your school belong?

It is as 'legitimate' to need help as it is 'legitimate' not to know everything! It's all right not to know!

There are people who surprise us no end with their incredibly vast knowledge. They seem to have swallowed the whole encyclopaedia and can recall any piece of information when required. They make wonderful after-dinner speakers and prove useful on the Trivial Pursuits team. Most of us, however, do not have this kind of memory, nor do we desperately want to have it. One is more likely to make a fool of oneself pretending to know something rather than admitting ignorance.

So much less pressure when you don't have to know it all!

Consider forgetting the need to be superhuman. Find someone who genuinely cares, who understands and is willing to listen, maybe even give advice... Trying to be a superman or a superwoman will eventually catch up with you. It often leads to heart attacks, nervous breakdowns, and complete burnout. You deserve better!

72

ASKING FOR HELP WHEN YOU NEED IT

When you admit you need help and support, does it feel as if you were admitting to incompetence?

Do you offer help to a colleague who seems to need it?

Since we all know that everybody needs help sometimes, what do you think you could do to create in your school a safe and supportive environment for yourself and others?

How do you feel about asking for help?
Jot down your thoughts:

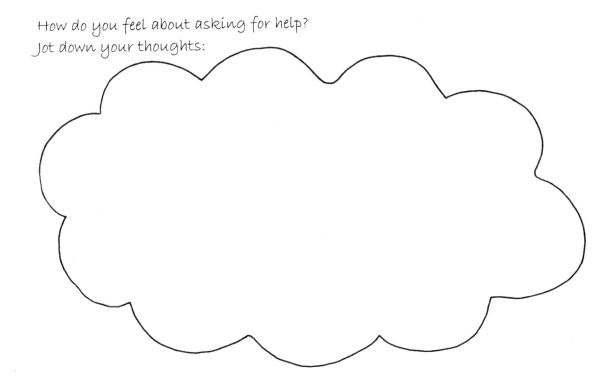

Making a shift from teaching the curriculum to teaching children

Any current curriculum will soon become obsolete, ministers of education will change, old programmes will lose validity and new ones will be introduced. If you always remember to teach the children, as opposed to teaching the programme, if you bear in mind that it is all about the children and for the children, you will be re-connected with your core which understands what your role, your mission really is.

Being fully alive in class

Can you think of a day when you didn't feel like working, when you let the day slip through your fingers, when you were half-heartedly going through the motions? I don't know anyone who has not had days like that.

It makes sense to make an effort, to bring your spark and enthusiasm into your work. It makes sense because only when we give our best can we enjoy work and feel good about ourselves.

Be fully alive in class for your own sake!

What does being fully alive in class mean to you?

Connection?
Creativity? Variety?
Challenge? Authenticity?
Humour? Excitement? Passion?

Listening to your inner voice

Start listening more attentively to your inner voice, your inner guide. Your true Self is the source of strength and wisdom and, as Parker J. Palmer* says, *it is a potential to be fulfilled, not a danger to be suppressed or an obstacle to be overcome.*

When we don't have confidence in our judgment, when we don't trust ourselves, our interactions with others come from a fearful place. We can make a decision to put fears aside and teach from more positive and liberating places within such as hope, empathy, curiosity, and honesty.

When we are in touch with our core, when we include our heart consciousness in our actions, we can re-claim courage to protect ourselves from negative influences and fly again!

Bringing more integrity to your life and work, bringing peace and joy to your soul is worth striving for.

REFLECT AND REVIEW

Browse again through your notes in the first two parts of the book.

What are the all-important things that stand out for you?

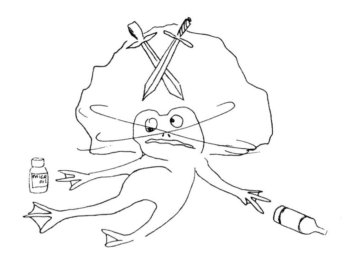

WHEN LIFE GETS TOUGH

Few people go through life without ever experiencing severe stress, feelings of burnout, depression, prolonged spells of apathy and low self-worth.

Have any of those experiences been a part of your life?

Most of us tend to see other people and events as causes of our stress: a partner who does not respect us, a child's rude remark, an unappreciative boss, a prolonged illness, a broken down car, a temperamental photocopier, a letter announcing the arrival of inspectors, an answering machine talking endlessly at you but still failing to give the information you need, and many others!

CAUSES OF STRESS

Think of the three things you see as the major causes of stress in your life:

Have you tried doing anything to reduce the effect of those stressful things?
Has it worked?

Under stress you probably experience some or all of the following symptoms:
fast heartbeat, waves of heat or cold going through your body, fast and shallow
breathing, sweaty palms, tense stomach, blurred vision, dry mouth.
And then in the long term: difficulties with sleeping, lack of appetite or constant
bingeing, problems with concentration, irritability.
Anything you would like to add?
Books devoted specifically to stress and ways of dealing with it will give you
detailed explanation of what exactly happens when your mind and body
experience excessive stress.

What is stress?
Here are two of many existing definitions:
> stress is a perceived inability to deal with a situation;
> stress is an emotional reaction to the perception that there are too many
> demands on too few resources.

The key word in both definitions is 'perception'. Although we are extremely
reluctant to accept that it is not the situation itself but the way we perceive it that
causes us to experience stress, I would like to invite you to give this idea serious
consideration.

When dealing with stress it is useful to look at it from two different angles:
- ♦   melting away the effects of stress we are already experiencing,
- ♦   changing our attitudes, and our perception of stressful situations.

Melting away the effects of stress we are already experiencing

DO AWAY WITH WEIGHTS

Imagine there are many weights in your life and work. Put labels
on them such as: disruptive Jamie, unfriendly colleague, a meeting
to attend, a difficult teenage son, etc., etc. The weights are on your
head, on your shoulders, attached to your hands and legs and keep
pulling you down draining your energy. It feels extremely
uncomfortable and painful to move.

Stand up, feeling the ground under your feet. Fill your lungs with
air and as you breathe out, shake all the weights off your body.
Imagine them falling off, one by one. Do it as many times as it
takes, and feel your body free and pleasantly light.

LOCK AWAY YOUR WORRIES

Sit down comfortably and breathe, in... out...

Imagine opening your head… gently taking out all the worrying thoughts and putting them into a drawer.
Open your heart and take out all the worrying feelings. Put them in the drawer with your thoughts and lock the drawer.

Now fill your mind with the picture of someone you love, of a beautiful sunrise, a meadow on a Spring morning...
Imagine a bird flying to you and giving you its wings. Instantly flap your wings and fly over the meadows, trees...
Fill your heart with joy and peace.

SWIM WITH DOLPHINS

Have you seen a documentary showing people swimming with dolphins? If this image appeals to you, let your mind take you there. The water is warm and carries you wherever you want to go. The gentle giants swim around you, jump out of the water inviting you to play. Feel light and playful and ecstatically happy.

For years I have observed staff rooms during breaks and have yet to see one person truly taking a break.

Next time you are in your staff room, take a look around: is anybody relaxing, focusing, stretching, breathing or doing anything which could be classified as taking a break? Pretty unlikely. Instead, clutching their coffee mugs and talking about work, people plump themselves into easy chairs (stomach squeezed and back slouched) in a stuffy room where windows are hardly ever opened.

Of course you want your coffee and of course certain things need to be discussed during breaks. However, I would like you to think about the possibility of extracting 30 seconds from your traditional break time

Here are three quick exercises for immediate relief of stress.

STOP AND BREATHE
(30 seconds - just for you)

Have a drink of water (sic!) or just a sip, if water is not your favourite thing.
Open the window or go out.
Drop your shoulders and let your arms hang loose.
Close your eyes (optional) and fill your lungs with air.
Slowly let the air out...
In, through the nose... and out through the mouth.
As you breathe in, imagine good energy coming through the top of your head.
As you breathe out, imagine all the tension leave your body and go into the ground.
Do this three times and join your colleagues with your mug of coffee for a chat.
30 seconds during every break - 30 seconds just for you.

Photocopy the picture on the next page and put it up on the wall as a reminder, until the exercise becomes a part of a your daily routine.

Stop and breathe...

SWITCH OFF
(1 minute, 3 x a day
- just for you)

If possible, have a sip of water and open the window.

Imagine there are switches in your brain, that can turn your thoughts 'on' and 'off'.
Close your eyes and fill your lungs with air...
Let the air out slowly...
'Go up to your brain' and turn all the switches off.

Every time you start thinking, go to that place in your brain and turn the appropriate switch off.
Breathe freely and continue gently switching off any thoughts that come.

COOK'S HOOK-P
(2 minutes - just for you)

When you're ready, slowly open your eyes.

This is one of a number of wonderful Brain Gym® (P. Dennison*) exercises.
The posture closes the electrical circuits in the body, and as a result contains and focuses disorganised by stress attention and energy.

Stand straight and breathe...
Stretch your arms in front of you, back of hands together, thumbs pointing down.
Still keeping your arms stretched out, thumbs down, cross right hand over left (or left over right) so palms are facing.
Interlock fingers and thumbs.
Turn wrists inwards and rest your hands on your chest.
Cross your legs (one ankle over the other).
Press your tongue against your palate.
Close your eyes and breathe deeply: in (through your nose)... and out (through your mouth)... in... and out...

When ready, uncross legs and arms. Touch fingertips of both hands together and breathe deeply for another minute.

Here are a few reminders how do deal with stress when you are ready to properly take care of yourself the way you deserve.

Exercise
Physical exercises help get rid of unwanted chemicals produced by stress. Unlike people in business, only a very small percentage of teachers seem to be exercising regularly. Make an effort to find some form of physical activity you enjoy. If you have fun with it, you will keep it up.

Take classes
Any classes you may enjoy: Yoga, Tai-Chi, massage, meditation, relaxation, painting, singing, bird watching, book binding. Remember, it has to be fun! Find a friend who will take the class with you. On a cold, winter night it takes a lot of determination to leave your cosy armchair and go out! It is good to have somebody who will motivate you to do it.

Sleep
Our resistance to negative effects of stress is dramatically reduced by lack of sleep. Unless you have small children, do make sure you get enough sleep! The importance of it cannot be over-emphasised!

Go to therapy
Many teachers I have come in contact with still see psychotherapy as some kind of an American whim; and not only therapy but any kind of professional help.
Accepting our limitations is as important as accepting our strengths. Remember that your endurance has its limits. If you feel you are on the verge of a breakdown, do not wait another day and find help!

Changing your perception of stress

along with some of your destructive attitudes and beliefs - an alternative way of dealing with stress.

Think once more of the three things that 'make' you feel stressed.
Why are they stressful? What do they MEAN to you? Be as specific as you can.

Accept for a moment (even if this does not sound convincing) that we ourselves give meaning to and make sense of our experience. Think about the things that cause you stress and ask yourself whether you are giving useful or destructive meaning to your experience.

The essence of this approach to stress is that
THE SOURCE OF STRESS IS INTERNAL, NOT E TERNAL.
In other words, what causes stress is not so much what happens but what it means to us, how we perceive it.

It is extremely uncomfortable for most of us to accept that we have control over our thinking, over the way we perceive potentially stressful events and the way we respond to them. We have control over our non-productive beliefs, such as:

I should be...
I should have done...
I ought to know...
I could never...

and have the power to change them into more reasonable and realistic ones.

EXERCISE THE POWER OF YOUR MIND

Think about a (potentially) stressful situation you have recently been in, maybe still are. Why is it stressful, what does it MEAN to you?
Accept for a moment (even if this does not sound convincing) that the person who gives sense to your experience is YOU.

Are you learning useful lessons from your stressful experience?

If not, try doing the following:
Sit in a chair, close your eyes and breathe deeply... in... out... in... out...
Imagine there is a screen on the wall opposite you.
The film you are going to watch is the situation in which you have recently experienced stress.

Feel your body supported by the chair... You are here.
The 'other you' is acting out the scene.
Watch it, breathing freely...

Now, with the enormous power your mind has, change the meaning the source of stress has for 'the other you', into a useful one. Take your time and when you're ready step into the screen and let the 'screen you' unite with the 'real you'.

Take a deep breath...
You are here, supported by the chair.

Remember, we are here to learn.
What lesson have you learned from the experience?

Keep your thoughts positive
because your thoughts become your words.

Keep your words positive
because your words become your actions.

Keep your actions positive
because your actions become your habits.

Keep your habits positive
because your habits become your values.

Keep your values positive
because your values become your future.

(Anon)

TRANSFORM YOUR MOOD

On the top row of faces mark the one that corresponds with the way you're feeling at the moment.

Close your eyes and breathe deeply.
  Remember a pleasant experience... a lovely place...
    How did you feel?...
      What did you see around you?...
        What sounds did you hear?...
  With every breath come closer to that wonderful space within yourself.

  Keep breathing and imagining yourself in this beautiful place,
  free of stress and worry.

Open your eyes.
  How does it feel now?... Are you a little calmer, a little happier?
  Has remembering something good put a smile on your face?

Now, mark your feelings on the bottom row of faces.

Think of the source of your stress. Does it appear equally bad or has something changed? Repeat the exercise until you feel considerably better.
It may be very challenging to find advantages in your stressful situation but if you keep looking you will eventually find them. It's worth the effort.

Burnout

Have you ever experienced burnout? Are you experiencing it now?
What does it feel like?

Most frequently we don't notice burnout approaching because we ignore the warning lights and the alarm bells. We are too busy, too preoccupied, too tired, too stressed out, too concerned with what is happening around us to stop and feel what is going on inside us.

...I simply have to do this work, it is my responsibility. Besides, if I don't do it, nobody will... So much depends on what I do and how I do it! So many people count on me and I mustn't disappoint them. If things go wrong, it will be my fault!... I have to find energy and time to handle things. I can't fail others and I can't fail myself... I have to be strong, everybody sees me as a strong person... Thinking about myself under the circumstances would be selfish and wrong. I can't appear to be a selfish, egocentric person... They need me!...

Does any of this sound familiar?

Teaching is a giving profession. We spend our lives nurturing our pupils, their hassled parents and our troubled colleagues. The children need us, their parents need us and our colleagues need us! Exhausted after a whole day at school we finally go home where our partners, children, elderly parents and friends need our time, our attention and energy. We are always expected to keep giving without end. And yet, do we always feel like it? How about when we are not well, not in the mood, worried about something, or simply really wanting to do something else?

Does anyone notice we are people too?

Do we notice it ourselves?

Whether or not our heart is open and ready to empathise and help, whether or not our mind is at rest and able to give attention and advice, we feel that things simply have to be done. So we do them.

The never-ending burden of demands on our time, attention, empathy, and energy, leads to exhaustion and frustration. As our hearts begin to close down, apathy, resignation, anger, and resentment creep in. All this, combined with our firm belief that we SHOULD be able to manage and stay in control, is a road to a nervous breakdown.

A nervous breakdown comes because we have chosen to ignore all the warning signs. It comes as an unwelcome but absolutely necessary lesson, which must be learned if we are to avoid a stroke, a heart attack or other serious illness.

The causes of burnout may be different for different people but for teachers with whom I have worked the ones most frequently experienced were:

- preparation, going through and counteracting the after-effects of gruelling inspections
- the inertia of the system and answering to individuals who do not always understand the complexity of educational issues
- the overwhelming bureaucracy and the amount of paperwork taking teachers away from teaching
- combining the demands of their private life with school paperwork
- lack of appreciation
- lack of inspiration
- caring for others while not caring for oneself
- lost, forgotten vision
- feelings of helplessness brought on by having to work in ways they believe to be wrong.

Burnout occurs as a result of acting one way and thinking another, or speaking one way and feeling another, or doing one thing and believing another. It requires a loot of energy to live with the emotional and mental fatigue created by lack of congruence.

Many teachers and headteachers feel that a tremendous amount of their energy goes into subtle manoeuvring. They desperately try to find ways of satisfying the authorities while giving children what they profoundly believe every child needs and deserves.

Nobody can tell you what to do to solve your dilemma. Some decisions you may have to make are risky and require courage and determination.

We don't always have the courage to go against the tide. Do not push yourself, the time may not be right.

You will know when you are ready.

Sometimes the dissonance becomes too strong to bear and we break down.

At the time it feels as if the world has collapsed around us. But when you start emerging from the dark hole, you will begin to understand that there is light out there!

The time of a breakdown is our time, our learning time, an opportunity for renewal.

What lessons have you learned from your breakdown (maybe a state of a 'near-breakdown') or from a breakdown of a colleague, a friend, a family member?

Teachers, some of them head teachers, have told me how important the experience has been to them.

They have learned about:

- the necessity to recognise and accept their limits
- the importance of releasing the need to be in control
- letting go of damaging, unrealistic beliefs
- forgiving themselves their mistakes, imperfections, doubt, resignation, impatience and anger
- the new experience of learning to be gentle with themselves and having compassion for themselves
- the need to admit they needed help!

As Ram Dass* says, through experiencing a breakdown and depression we are given a chance to reach a deeper sense of who we are, and discover how much more we have to give.

We may discover that we need a big change of career, a new way of life. We may discover that we wish to continue teaching, recognising the indisputable need to take care of ourselves while taking care of others.

There is another lesson to be learned, crucial for those who decide to stay within the system and continue teaching. Every system has rules and regulations, inspectors and committees, targets, requirements, expectations and ways of measuring performance. The rules may or may not be applicable to our situation.

The system will change. In a few years the rules will be different, inspectors will go and others will take their place. However, your integrity and your sense of self-worth must always be protected.

Negativity

There is (...) a highly infectious mental and social disease in our society which I call 'gloomeritis'. The more you talk about gloom, the more gloom there is to talk about.

(R. Holden*)

Remember your first days of teaching? Was the staff room atmosphere uplifting, energising and supportive, or was it heavy, gloomy and generally negative?

What is your staff room like now? How do you think a new teacher would react to it?

If negativity is the accepted behaviour, new teachers will feel obliged to behave the same way. Their high energy and fresh enthusiasm will struggle to remain alive. Not a good start but for many it is everyday reality. From day one many easily influenced young teachers become victims of this self-inflicted pattern of behaviour.

New staff induction day

I once gave my university students an unusual assignment: I asked them to stop complaining and criticising anybody and anything for three hours and to write about their experience. At the time nobody, including myself, realised how extremely challenging the task was going to prove.

Have you ever tried to stop criticising and complaining for any length of time? If not, I invite you to carry out the experiment. What you can discover is fascinating!

Complaints and criticism pour out of most of us. We may not always say everything we are thinking but we do so internally. If you kept a log of your daily complaints and criticisms, how many do you think you would record a day?

We complain about the government, the system and regulations, about the children and non-supportive parents, about the head, our colleagues, about the mess, the food in the canteen, etc., etc.

Well, that list can get pretty long.

Complaints and criticisms create truly toxic matter, which poisons our minds and hearts. Negativity is a habit; it is a way of feeling, thinking, a way of being. When on a perfectly good day somebody asks us how we are, we often answer: '*not too bad*', '*plodding along*', '*mustn't grumble*', as if: '*very well, thanks*' was not good enough!

I have had colleagues who simply wallowed in negativity: criticising and complaining seemed to be their favourite pastime! When somebody suggested solutions or offered help, their reactions were quite predictable:

> *I tried that and it didn't work...*
> *That could never work for me...*
> *It's not in my personality to do that...*
> *Nothing new - I have done that and nothing happened...*
> *YES, BUT...*
> *The inspectors won't like it...*
> *The Head will not agree...* etc.

Do you enjoy wallowing in negativity or would you rather get out of it?
Do you see negativity as harmless or destructive?

Are you willing to look at alternative ways of being and to introduce some changes into your behaviour? If your answer is YES, try the following exercises. (D. Firth*)

Think of a challenging situation.
If you'd taken a pill that allowed you to see only the positive aspects of this situation, what would you see?

Do it a few times to get the hang of it. Make a habit of this way of thinking. This may feel extremely uncomfortable at first but trust me, if you practice long enough it will become your new way of being, leading to better mental and physical health and a much more pleasant life.

Your very thought leaves a mark in your brain by creating a neural connection. When you repeat the same thought, you create a neural pathway that gets stronger and more established with every repetition. Be careful what you choose to think.

You can choose to be open-minded or close-minded,
to think independently or sheepishly copy others,
to be optimistic and positive, or pessimistic and miserable.

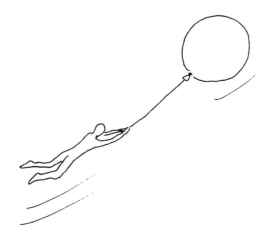

It is of paramount importance to choose carefully what you think because

you will never go higher
than your thoughts.

Make a decision to stop criticising and complaining for any length of time (two hours, a day, a week) and reflect:

♦   has it made any difference to the way you feel?

♦   has it influenced the way you relate to others?

♦   has it influenced your way of thinking about issues or people?

If you decide to start choosing more positive thoughts while attempting to eliminate the negative ones, I suggest you try the following:
every time you catch yourself thinking a negative thought,

- imagine it written on a whiteboard - take a sponge, erase the thought and in its place write a positive one
- imagine it written on your computer screen and say to yourself: 'delete, delete' and replace it with a positive thought. (J. Canfield*)

N.B. It is essential you put a positive thought in the place of the negative one. Your brain does not like a vacuum and if there is nothing to replace the negativity, it will soon bring the unwanted thought back.

The purpose of this exercise is not to turn you into a 'Happy-go-Lucky Silly Billy' but to help you become more conscious of the way you think and of the effects negativity has on you. And, in case you wonder, this is not about constructive criticism. It is about bitching, moaning and groaning, which drain your energy, get you into a pattern of negativity, while changing absolutely nothing!
Joining the negativity club drains you of life supporting energy and sends you on a downward spiral ending in complete exhaustion and no accomplishment!

It is so easy to go deeper and deeper into a pool of negativity, complaints and criticism and to sink into it without even realising it. Put space between yourself and the problems you are attempting to solve.

Defend yourself against negativity of others

NEGATIVITY IS CONTAGIOUS!

Distance yourself, both physically and mentally, from the toxic pool of negativity. Jumping into it with the people you are supporting will help nobody!
You need to have plenty of support and learn effective ways of protecting yourself against the frustration and aggression of angry children at school, some of their demanding, constantly complaining parents, discontented and negative colleagues, as well as against unappreciative and over-critical family members and anybody who throws their negativity at you.

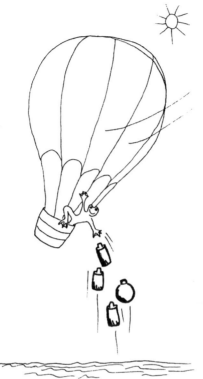

Read the next two chapters of this book and do the exercises. Buy and read self-help books, go on retreats, join a support group. And if you can't find one, start your own! Whenever possible, surround yourself with positive, optimistic people. To be caring, giving and nurturing, and yet remain sane and healthy yourself, focus on the people and issues while discarding the destructive content of the toxic negativity pool.

You can benefit from your stressful experiences. You can learn to make a decision to change your state of mind and to change the way you perceive situations. For most of us it takes time and effort for this way of thinking to become a habit. You can, however, help yourself when you know what to do, and when you fully appreciate the power of your mind.

When you become aware of your thinking patterns and decide to make positive changes, you are already on the way to a more fulfilling life.

Just remember to act from the heart.

INVITE CHANGE INTO YOUR LIFE

In the previous chapter

I have invited you to consider the view that stress is caused primarily by the way we perceive and interpret the situation

I have suggested you accept your needs as equally important as the needs of others

I have asked you to understand that your vulnerability is human and that admitting you need help and support is in fact a sign of strength rather than weakness

I have suggested that you have power to take responsibility for the way you think and feel.

All or some of those suggestions may sound and feel extremely uncomfortable, challenging, even frightening. They will require deep thought and if you decide they make sense to you, will call for a change of attitudes, beliefs and often life-long habits.

Clasp your palms together and interlock your fingers.
Which thumb is on top? Right? Left?
Doesn't matter…
Now straighten your fingers and slide your palms as if you were opening a fan, so that when you interlock your fingers again the other thumb is on top. How does that feel? Awkward, strange, uncomfortable?…
Interestingly enough, if you were to keep interlocking your fingers the 'new' way for about three weeks, the feeling of discomfort would disappear.
(That is, unless you decided to continue feeling uncomfortable!)

Change, any kind of change, is bound to trigger emotions: fear, excitement, anxiety, anticipation, awkwardness, discomfort. The feelings may be generally negative or predominantly positive but most have an underlying fear of the unknown.

Think about the change you experience in your life: change in the weather, changing trains, changing the style of the clothes you wear, your address, your car, the country you live in, your partner, your doctor, your way of thinking, your attitude, your political orientation, the supermarket where you do your weekly shopping.

Close your eyes and think about any of the above changes. How does the thought about change make you feel?

One thing is certain: the only constant we have is change.

The sooner we accept the absolute fact that change will occur whether we like it or not, whether we accept it or not, whether we 'permit' it or not, the better our chance to avoid a waste of energy, disappointment, frustration and futile struggle to prevent change from happening.
We may succeed in delaying change, re-directing its course but never in stopping it.

We are living in times of unprecedented speed of change. Think about the generation of your parents and their parents. What was life like for them? Most of them mastered some kind of skill in their youth and then went on applying it for the rest of their working life. Children lived the way their parents lived, and their children lived very similar lives.
This is no longer so.

The only constant we have is change

Think of all the things you have had to learn in the last two, three years. It is quite a long list for most of us.

Learning new skills throughout life has become an undisputed necessity for anybody wanting to keep pace with the rapidly changing world.

There is little doubt that the speed of change has gone through the roof!

Because of that, helping young people develop confidence in their ability to learn, to think, and to respond effectively to change is now of paramount importance.

This means that we, teachers, must have a futuristic outlook. We need to start by taking a good look at the way we respond to change ourselves before we can effectively guide others.

In the times of drastic change it is the learner who will inherit the future. The learned will find himself equipped for the world that no longer exists.

(E. Hoffer*)

The first purpose of our considerations is to suggest you look closely at your attitude to change and the ways you approach it.

The second is to invite you to explore and develop more effective and enjoyable strategies that will make life easier and lead to more creativity, more fulfilment, and more fun.

Do you agree with any of the following?

A change imposed is a change opposed.

You can never change another person; you can only change yourself, your attitude, your belief, your behaviour.

Successful people don't just accept change, they embrace it.

Instead of resisting often inevitable change, it may make better sense to start looking for advantages it brings with it.

Think for a moment about some significant changes in your life.

1.

2.

3.

4.

5.

6.

Which have been imposed on you?

Which have 'just happened'?

Which have been the results of your decision?

It may be interesting to see whether any one of the three 'change patterns' dominates your life. However, there is no need to make a value judgment about the way change occurs. The important question is whether you are happy with the way change has taken place in your life.

How do you most frequently respond to change?

1. Do you resist change and dig your heels in, refusing to move?

If you are like most of us, you find change frightening, awkward, anxiety producing, at best uncomfortable. Even when we are not happy with things, we prefer them to stay the way they are. We assume that change will either not help or make things worse. Our attitudes are reflected in the language we use: since *better the devil we know*, we *let sleeping dogs lie* and do our best *not to rock the boat.*

It has often been said that repeating the same behaviour will just get you the same results.

Think of a problem that was bothering you for a long time. Your 'gut feeling', was screaming at you that something needed to be done, yet you continued to act and react in the same old, familiar ways expecting a different outcome!

We are intelligent people, understanding the principle of cause and effect, yet we tend to ignore reality, refuse to live consciously and instead, settle for: 'something will eventually happen and things will get better'.
Why do we do it? Why do we stubbornly refuse to move?
We are afraid of the unknown, so we expect things to become worse rather than better and stay put, be it

in a job we don't find satisfying,
in a house surrounded with
    unfriendly neighbours,
in a no longer functional
    relationship,
in sticking to an unproductive way
    of thinking,
in holding on to a destructive
    attitude, belief or a 'well tested'
    way of doing things.

Has it ever happened to you that you knew something was profoundly wrong but you made every possible effort to convince yourself that things were not really that bad?...

We often live with our heads in the sand hoping that if we wait long enough, some day we will find a magic pill which will make people and situations change painlessly to our advantage. This could mean a very long wait.

2. Do you resign yourself to change?

'There is nothing I can do about it, I will have to plod on the best I can'
If this is what you tend to say to yourself, do you think this attitude works for you? Being 'resigned to your fate' may save you energy but does it help you feeling content with life?

3. Do you accept change and do your best to see the benefits it can potentially bring?

Accepting change doesn't necessarily mean that you don't feel any apprehension or fear. You do, however, make an effort to turn it to your advantage.
If you can't beat them, join them. Do you recognise yourself in this statement?

This brings us to the fourth way of dealing with change, not responding or reacting to change already occurring but actively LOOKING FOR IT.

4. Are you pro-actively looking for opportunities to instigate change?

This attitude involves thinking of ways to improve aspects of your life with which you are not content. While realising that change is inevitable, it also means taking responsibility for the way you live. In other words, taking things into your own hands, rather than waiting for someone else to do it.

Have you had the experience of making a conscious effort to bring about changes? Not necessarily because something wasn't working but because you thought that trying a new approach would be exciting and could lead to even better results.

STRETCHING YOUR BOUNDARIES

When you decide to get used to changing things:

1. Buy a different brand of soap.
2. Do your shopping in a supermarket you have never been to.
3. Buy three things you have never bought before.
4. In the staff room, sit in a different chair.
5. Go home taking a different route.
6. Watch a TV programme you have always refused to watch.

Think of more fun ways of getting used to changing things. Do one little exercise every day. Have fun!

If you are happy with the way in which you have dealt with change in your life, great. If not, the good news is:

You can change the way you deal with change!

getting used to changing things...

CELEBRATING YOUR LIFE

Write a speech you would like someone to make about you and your life at a party to celebrate your 70th birthday. What would you like the person to say about you?

Think what things you must change (or continue doing!) in your life in order to achieve what you want to be remembered for.

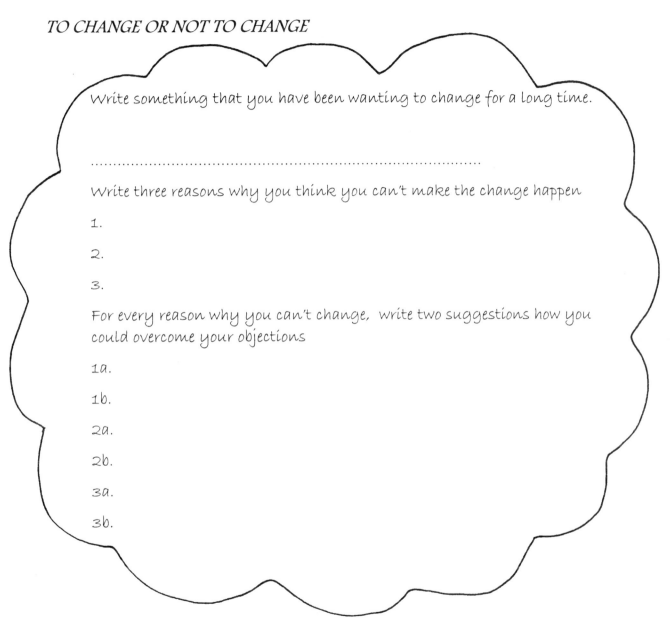

Write something that you have been wanting to change for a long time.

....

Write three reasons why you think you can't make the change happen

1.

2.

3.

For every reason why you can't change, write two suggestions how you could overcome your objections

1a.

1b.

2a.

2b.

3a.

3b.

Has this exercise altered the way you perceive obstacles to change?

Some changes are enjoyable, some are painful and truly difficult. Whatever they are, remember there is always something good that will eventually emerge, even if you cannot see it at the time.

Think of five things you want to be different in your life.

	What do I want to change?	What do I want things to be?	What do I need to do for the change to happen?
1			
2			
3			
4			
5			

your will is the magical force that can make things change

you can do it; the choice is yours

Complete the exercise with all the things you want to be different.
Now look at your answers and ask yourself one last question:

Am I ready and willing to make the changes now or is the time not quite right yet?

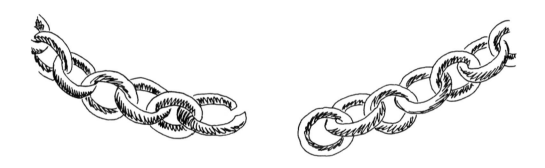

Some changes require a lot of time so don't let anyone push you into doing something for which you are not ready.

If you allow yourself quiet time and listen to your heart, you will know when to take action.

LIVE YOUR LIFE TO THE FULL

The challenge set before us is not only to exist but to live fully.

(R. Holden*)

Life or survival?

Not living life to the full seems to be a terrible waste, yet many people I know resign themselves to the idea that life is tough and settle for mere survival.

Refuse to settle for surviving!
Next time you find yourself among people (in a meeting,
at a conference, or a training programme) look at their faces.
Do they emanate joy, enthusiasm and interest,
or disillusionment, bitterness and resignation?

Has anything been stopping you from living your life fully?

THOU
SHALT
DO IT
LATER.

Maybe you have been saying to yourself things like:

...when I finish that job...
...when I move house...
...when the children grow up...
...when I get this promotion...
...when I complete this project...
...when the inspectors have done their job and gone...
...when this term finishes...
...when..., then I will be able to start living...

Life's challenges will never be completed for as long as you are alive. Your life is happening while you're finishing that job, while you are planning to move house, while somebody is considering your promotion, while you are waiting for the inspectors to arrive and while your children are growing up.
Stop this self-defeating perpetuation of mere survival (if this is what you have been doing) and START LIVING TODAY.

Today is the first day of the rest of your life

Take time to love and be loved - it is one of life's greatest glories
Take time to listen - it is the path to true understanding
Take time to talk - it is the way to unburden your heart
Take time to be with yourself - it is the source of power
Take time to work - it is the way to fulfilment
Take time to play - it is the secret of staying young
Take time to read - it is the fountain of wisdom and fun
Take time to laugh - it is the music of the soul
Take time to dream - it is your road to the stars!

(adapted from a poem 'Time' - author unknown)

What is life truly about for you?

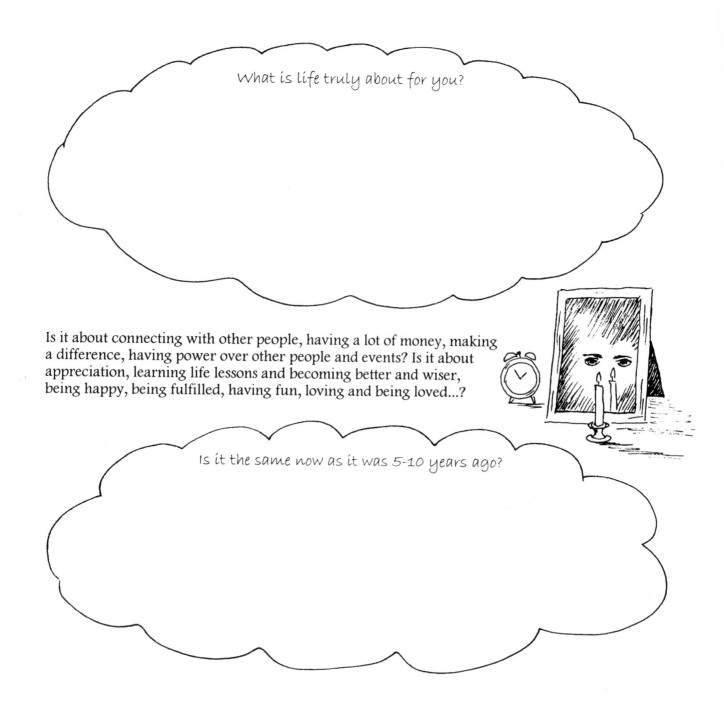

Is it about connecting with other people, having a lot of money, making a difference, having power over other people and events? Is it about appreciation, learning life lessons and becoming better and wiser, being happy, being fulfilled, having fun, loving and being loved...?

Is it the same now as it was 5-10 years ago?

Taking charge of your life

Whatever your life is like now, it is helpful to bear in mind that you can change it.

As Holden elegantly puts it,

life is a conscious, creative act - you have the power to create and re-create it again and again.

(R. Holden*)

Learn to understand and appreciate the brain-programming power of your thought.

Think again about some aspect of your life which needs changing.

Write it in first person, present tense, as if what you want was already true.

For example:

I am confidently handling my colleagues' criticism.

I am easily, openly and firmly defending my opinions.

Repeat the sentence every morning and every evening. It is most likely that you will soon notice a change in the way you act and feel about your challenge.

Always bear in mind that any thought, good or bad, which you repeat over and over again becomes your subconscious programme.

Is life about being happy?

Many of us believe that life is about happiness, yet we often find it difficult to say what exactly happiness means to us. If you don't know what happiness means to you, how will you know whether you are happy or not?

If you asked ten people you know pretty well whether they consider themselves happy, how many do you think would give an unqualified, positive answer?

Try conducting a little experiment. Copy the questionnaire below and give it to a few people, asking them to answer the three questions (anonymously, if you/they prefer).

Please answer the following questions:	
Do you consider yourself happy?	
Why?	
If not, what do you think you would need to be a happy person?	

My experience is that most people give qualifying answers, such as,

I am happy when...
I would be happy if…
I will be happy provided…

Many don't see themselves as happy at all. If you carry out your little research project, you will find out that the answers have little to do with people's looks, financial situation, fame, or work success.

Always be aware of the power of your thought *

* Your thought is the genie of your lamp

I am happy because
I have made up my mind to be happy

Happiness is a matter of decision, a decision that needs to be made every morning. The thought that you choose your attitude, that you decide how you feel, is very uncomfortable for most of us to accept. It may take time to think and re-think it, to digest it, to argue with it, and reject it before you learn to accept it. The moment you do, you give up being a victim of circumstances and gain the only true power, your self-power. You begin to understand that your destiny is in your hands.

My attitude to life determines my destiny

Letting go

Let go of everything that stops you from living your life to the full

Letting go is about getting rid of tension, worry and anxiety, of different kinds of addictions, of the need to have more and be more. It is about becoming free, light, open to new experiences, peaceful, and calm. Doesn't this sound inviting?

Let go of the need to be perfect

Do you know anybody who is? Why do you think you of all people should be perfect? Doesn't it make more sense to always do the best you can?

Let go of the need to know it all

Admitting you don't know everything and being willing to find out and learn is a liberating experience for those of us hooked on knowing all the answers. There is no chance you will ever know everything.
Get rid of the need and enjoy the excitement of the life-long learning.

Let go of rigidity

What is rigid can easily break. It is flexibility that allows a young tree to withstand strong winds.
Rigidity means closing your mind to anything that may upset your established order.
The opposite of rigidity is an open mind and the ability to change.

Have you noticed any rigidity in your attitudes?

Let go of trying too hard

Think of the last time you forgot the name of somebody you know pretty well. You were getting more and more irritated, desperately trying to dig the name out of your memory. All in vain. Eventually you gave up and sat down to watch television. And suddenly, half way through the film - snap, the name jumped out at you.

Often trying hard does not bring expected results. The more effort we put into something, the more we push ourselves or others, the further we seem to be from our goal. Think about it.

Trying hard frequently results in stress blocks and in getting stuck. Something doesn't work so, instead of looking for alternative ways of doing it, we stubbornly do more of the same. Next time you are tempted to 'try harder', replace it by 'doing your best' or 'trying smarter'.

When you try too hard, you often make a mess of things.

When you do your best and let go of the result, things have a chance to flow easily.

Let go of unnecessary baggage

If your house is like the houses most of us live in, it is full of:
- books and magazines you will never read again
- files you will never open again
- pots and pans you will never cook in again
- tapes and records you will never listen to again
- clothes you will never wear again.

Why do we store all this baggage?
Is it the fear of lack? 'I don't need it now but one day I may...'
Things give many people the feeling of security. Do you know people who go away for a weekend and take with them enough stuff to last them a month - just in case?
This kind of baggage drags you down, makes your movements heavy and slow.
Can you imagine how you would it feel if you got rid of all this unnecessary baggage? Think about it and, if you decide this is right for you, start emptying your drawers.

Let go of the need to control

When in class we need to be in control or else the children will walk all over us. This useful professional skill tends to spill over onto our lives outside school. We may easily become true control freaks wanting to take charge of other peoples' lives, their thinking, their emotions and their behaviour. Does that sound familiar?

The need to control is a big weight to carry around. Controlling others more often than not results in alienation, broken friendships, hurt and anger.

Other people have their own journey, their own purpose in life. Rather than trying to change them, let them be, let them make their own mistakes and learn their own lessons. They need to become who they are meant to become.

Let go of your anger and resentment

Our minds are often cluttered with anger, resentment, blame and self-criticism.

Why do we hang on to those destructive thoughts and feelings? Is it because they are familiar or in some strange way gratifying?

I know people who carry grudges all their lives and sometimes take them to their grave. What a burden it is! The anger and resentment you feel for other people eats YOU up, not them.

Think about it and when you are ready, make a list of people with whom you have fallen out. Then pick one and decide what kind of action you will take: write a letter, make a phone call, then do it!

Forgiveness sets you free.

Let go of the addiction to work

When you notice that you're working all the hours God has given, ask yourself:
Why am I doing this?
Is it a sense of duty, love of the job, an absolute necessity, or am I escaping from some pain or emptiness in my life?
Is it my need to identify with the work I do or am I substituting something that is missing in my life?
Is it the need to stay in control, is it my perfectionism or haven't I noticed that
THERE IS LIFE OUTSIDE THE SCHOOL BUILDING?

Bring more fun into your life

Is fun in your life restricted to parties and an occasional night out?

Many of us were brought up to believe that life is tough and work is a serious business not to be enjoyed.

Have Victorian 'truths' such as *no pain no gain, hard work and suffering will take you to the Kingdom of Heaven, grit your teeth and get on with the job* influenced your beliefs about work?

Does your view of professionalism conflict with the notion that work can be fun?

If you are not making your life enjoyable, you are depriving yourself of happy moments, of feeling positive energy flow, of the exciting sense of fulfilment. You are also depriving those coming in contact with you of your positive vibes.

If you wish to explore ways of bringing more fun and enjoyment into your work, join me in some daily fun practice. Amazing, as it may seem, even enjoying life needs practice.

Trying out each and every exercise will help you decide which are the ones you want to make a part of your daily life.

Enjoy your life,
don't let it pass you by...

FUN PRACTICE 1   Put a smile on your face

Carry out a little experiment. Ask somebody to take two pictures of you: one with a solemn, worried face and the other with a smile. Look at those two pictures: which person would you rather spend your time with?

Many people identify respect, authority, responsibility, and discipline with a stern, serious expression on their face, sometimes accompanied by a detached and pompous way of addressing people.

Some teachers are wonderfully playful by nature, while some of us are not. If you are like I am, not playful by nature, I suggest you nevertheless allow others to be. Laugh at their jokes and take in their lightness.

Playfulness can be present in very serious learning (P. Metz*), and it is so much more enjoyable! Humour relaxes the brain and gets rid of learning blocks. Things that are funny will be remembered.

When you feel you are ready to try humour and playfulness, just allow it to happen. When the atmosphere around you lightens up, when you give yourself permission to smile and laugh, you will begin to feel lighter too.

FUN PRACTICE 2 Step back and watch learning unfold

Stop trying hard, whatever you are doing, and
let things unfold. We teachers try too hard!
What is more, we see trying even harder as
beneficial and requiring appreciation. The
border-line between making people aware of
things, creating an environment in which they
will experience learning, and pushing
information down their throats, is often quite
subtle. It is amazing what can happen when we
allow learning to happen rather than forcing it,
pushing it, trying harder...

Next time you have a chance, put all the effort
into preparing your lesson and creating an exciting learning environment.
Then, withholding all judgment and expectations, watch the learning happen.
Observe the children.
Observe yourself.

Write about the experience.

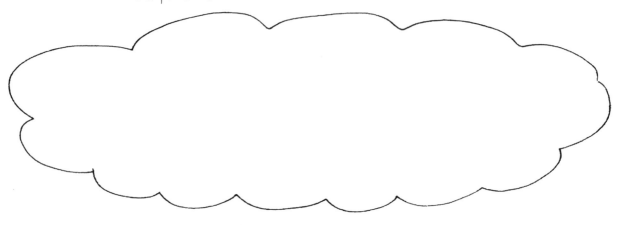

FUN PRACTICE 3   Decide to have a good day today!

 There are days when most of us may find it impossible to keep above the troubled waters. There are, however, many, many more that could be much better, if only we would put effort into making them better!

Here are a few suggestions for you to consider.
Try some out, that is if you are not doing them already!

A. A fun-only pretend-telescope
Take this telescope with you to work and view every event through it. Unlike your rose-tinted spectacles you will only be able to focus on the funny, amusing and light side of things.

B. Surprise niceness
On the way to work think
of one person you will do
something nice for,
for no reason at all.
And do it...

C. Discover a person
Make one attempt a day to connect with somebody. Choose a person you don't know well and do your best to discover as much as possible about their life, their likes and dislikes, their interests and challenges. Be fascinated by people, in particular the people you do not naturally attract you. You may be truly surprised by what you discover.

D. *Make a poster*
for yourself to remind you about the important things in your life. You can choose any of the 'golden thoughts' in this book or write your own.

My recent posters say:

Today I appreciate and enjoy every person I meet

Smile every hour, on the hour

E. *Daily plan*
Before you make a list of things 'TO DO', make a list of things that will help you enjoy the day. Make a practice list here:

....

....

....

....

....

....

....

Let it become a habit.
It does brighten the day!

FUN PRACTICE 4   *Become more creative*

Schooling and upbringing often stifle our natural creativity. We begin to draw like others, dance like others, dress like others...
Being creative keeps us fully alive and it is fun!
If you think that you are not a creative person, you are wrong! The essential thing to discover your creativity is to suspend all judgment and give yourself permission to go with the flow.

Here are a few hints how you can release the creative You.

A. *Be a creative cook*
If you tend to follow recipes, just for once don't! Make a dish using your imagination, something you have never made before. Be brave! The worst that can happen is that you will have to eat it all by yourself or throw it in the bin. So what?!

B. *Be a creative gardener*
Change a small part of the landscape of your garden. Follow any wild dream regarding the shape of the flowerbeds and the plants in them.

C. *Be a creative writer*
Think of something you would like to teach your children, e.g. how to be appreciative or the value of being truthful, patient. Now write a story illustrating what you want to teach.

D. *Be a creative decorator*
Visit a junk shop and buy an old piece of furniture. Get a few small tins of paint (choose your favourite colours) and paint the piece without using stencils or patterns. Be free, do what your heart tells you to do. You will be surprised how satisfying it can be.

E. *Be a creative artist*
Buy some poster paints and paint a picture of your mood. Cover the whole page with colour. Feel free and light and let your hand guide you. It does not matter whether anybody will like your picture or not. All that matters is the fun you will have, and your feeling of freedom.

Do one creative thing a week and surprise yourself with all the things you can do and never even thought you could.

Think of all the things you have always wanted to do. Pick one and do it NOW!

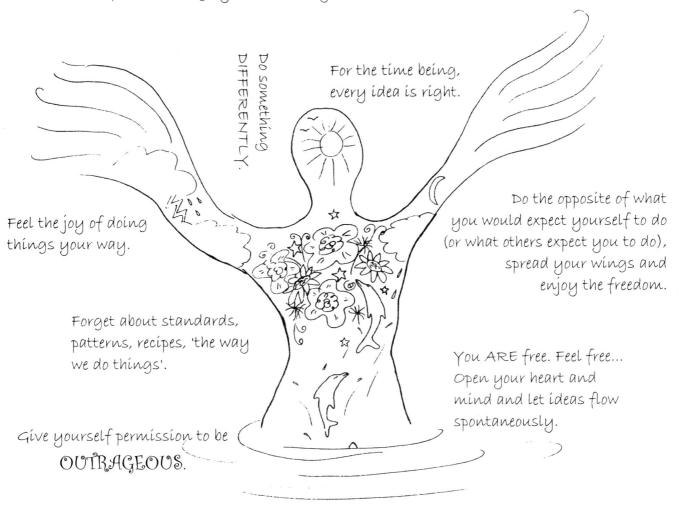

Do something DIFFERENTLY.

For the time being, every idea is right.

Feel the joy of doing things your way.

Do the opposite of what you would expect yourself to do (or what others expect you to do), spread your wings and enjoy the freedom.

Forget about standards, patterns, recipes, 'the way we do things'.

You ARE free. Feel free... Open your heart and mind and let ideas flow spontaneously.

Give yourself permission to be OUTRAGEOUS.

Temporarily suspend all judgment and critical evaluation of what you do. For the time being they are OUT OF PLACE.

Be brave - step outside your comfort zone.

The time has come to sum it all up.
You might want to browse through the pages of this book again and think about ...

Make some picture posters and hang them in your room to remind yourself about your decisions, and anything you want to remember. We all need constant reminders!

It's much easier to make changes with a friend who can support you on your way to a happier life; a person who can listen, who is ready to suspend judgment and, ideally, share your thoughts and feelings.
But it is possible to do it all on your own.

Don't waste your life feeling miserable!
Mostly it is a question of appreciating the incredible power of your mind and making a conscious decision to be happy.

Enjoy and appreciate who you are and what you do.
Enjoy and appreciate the people in your life who help you feel fulfilled.

From the bottom of my heart I wish you wisdom and determination in all your endeavours.

Books you may like to read

Jack Black, *Mind Store.* Harper Collins, 1994
Nathaniel Branden, *Six Pillars of Self-Esteem*, 1994
Jack Canfield, *How to Build Your Self-Esteem* (audio tapes)
Ram Dass and Paul Gorman, *How Can I Help.* Alfred A. Knopf, NY 1987
David Firth, *How to Make Work Fun.* Gower, 1995
Carla Hannaford, *Awakening the Child Heart.* Jamilla Nur Publishing, 2002
Robert Holden, *Living Wonderfully.* Thorsons, 1994
Susan Jeffers, *End the Struggle and Dance with Life.* Hodder & Stoughton, 1996
Spencer Johnson, *Who Moved My Cheese.* GP Putnam's Sons, NY 1998
Blaine Lee, *The Power Principle.* A Fireside Book, Simon & Schuster, 1998
Andrew Matthews, *Follow Your Heart.* Seashell Publishers, 1997
Pamela Metz, *The Tao of Learning.* Humanics New Age, 1995
Parker J. Palmer, *The Courage to Teach.* Jossey-Bass Inc., 1998
Jane Revell & Susan Norman, *In Your Hands.* Saffire Press, 1998
Pamela Sims, *Awakening Brilliance.* Bayhampton Publications, 1997

Eva Hoffman PhD has been a teacher and a teacher educator for over 30 years. Her doctoral dissertation was one of the earliest pieces of research focused on accelerated learning.

As a 'hands-on' educational consultant she remains as busy as ever. Travelling extensively she passionately promotes a more heart-and-mind-friendly approach to teaching and learning.

Winner of the Family Learning Millennium Award, she is involved in numerous projects maintaining close links with many educational organisations all over the world. She lives in Cheshire, UK.

Other titles by Eva Hoffman:

'The Learning Adventure'   - ISBN 0953538702
'A Guide to The Learning Adventure'   - ISBN 0953538710
'My First Book Of Abundance'   - ISBN 0953538761

'Introducing Children To ...'   - Series ISBN 095353877X
     ... Their Amazing Brains' - ISBN 0953538753
     ... Their Senses'   - ISBN 0953538737
     ... Their Intelligences'   - ISBN 0953538729
     ... Mind Mapping'   - ISBN 0953538745